Rose Petals for Josephine

by
Nigel Walker

Kobalt Books
St. Louis / Philadelphia

To the "Josephine" of my life, whoever it may be.

© 2007 by Nigel Walker

ISBN: 978-0-9769117-6-0 (**10-digit ISBN:** 0-9769117-6-0)

All rights reserved. No part of this book may be reproduced, stored in a retrieval system, or transmitted by any means, electronic, mechanical, photocopying, recording, or otherwise, without written permission from the author.

No liability is assumed with respect to the use of the information contained herein. Although every precaution has been taken in preparation of this book, the publisher and author assume no responsibility for errors or omissions. Neither is any liability assumed for damages resulting from the use of the information contained herein.

For information:
Kobalt Books
P.O. Box 1062,
Bala Cynwyd, PA 19004
Printed in the U.S.A
www.kobaltbooks.com

Cover Design by Thomas Roach

Published by Kobalt Books L.L.C.
An original publication of Kobalt Books L.L.C.

INTRODUCTION	7
At First Sight	9
World Wonder	10
Scandalous	11
When I Pursue a Woman	12
One Condition	13
Daydreams	15
Night Vision	16
The Lady's Answer	17
F. L. O. W.	18
Love Theory	19
Love Law (Love Infinity)	20
How I Felt on 02-06-04	21
(On the Surface)	21
How I Felt on 02-06-04	22
(Deep Within)	22
When I Get You Alone	23
Feeling You	24
Acts of Nature	26
As We Continue – The Morning After	28
The Climax	29
Disconnected	30
The Seasons Haiku	32
The Present Matters	33
My Love Theme	34
Why I Kept Calling	36
Why I Haven't Called in a While	37
Anti-Social	38
Why I'm not the Perfect Guy	39
My Love in Return	41
Feeling You Still	43
LSD (Love So Deep)	44
Taken	45
My Paradise	46

- I. C. U. 47
- The Truth about Relationships 48
- The New Years' Eve 49
- Long Eyes 51
- My Poem Cry 52
- No Grudges 54
- In Time… 55
- Visions of Rapture 56
- Marooned Visions 58
- Words Never Said… 59
- A Lifetime 61
- Rose Petals for Josephine 62
- A Bit of Wishful Thinking 64
- You Simply Are… 65
- Unconventional 66
- Untitled (Cyberchat) 67
- Volatile Affections 68
- Got Me Looking So Crazy in Love 69
- Right Here, Right Now 70
- Window to the Soul 71
- ABOUT THE AUTHOR 72

INTRODUCTION

Rose Petals for Josephine is the second volume of the *Secret Diaries of Jean Batiste*, a book of a hopeless romantic who dedicated his heart and poems to the women of his life. Within this next chapter, one of the women dedicated in the *Secret Diaries* is taken from the multitude and placed on personal public display. An in-depth look is given to the relationship between Jean and his named love interest, Josephine, to whom the entire book is dedicated. It chronicles the trials of love and loss, and his feelings of the entire affair. Throughout the ups and downs of love, Jean Batiste desperately seeks an answer to his questionable romantic endeavors as he plucks...*Rose Petals for Josephine.*

At First Sight

She crept into my memory like silk stalkings;
Smooth and without much effort;
Flaunting a sexual attitude that was never subtle;
And without rebuttal,
I stayed in silence and played into the sway that shaped her slow motion approach;
I tried to show no intimidation,
But her presence made the very nature of my existence unstable;

If there is a smile that can launch a thousand ships,
Hers has the power to lead them home;
I felt all alone in a world that spun out of control as she strolled within a whisper's distance.
It was this instance that changed me;
For I never knew that my heart could be stolen so easily;
But I could hear the beat fade as she proceeded to pass me by;
She then looks back with a passionate sparkle in her eyes,
Glowing in the acknowledgement of knowing that she was in control of me…

World Wonder

She was a sophisticated lady with a natural beauty
Straight from the motherland;
With a genuine complexion, smooth as the sandy surface of glorious shores;
And a smile to cue the heavens to chorus.
Sexuality accented her vocabulary,
Balanced with similar substance in her stroll;
A physical wonder of the world and indeed a fitting mold;
Filled to the edge of perfection with no room for defect and I beg of her to…
"Please come my way!"

Scandalous

She's so scandalous
when she makes me confess
that I stare at her chest
As she offers the gesture
that it is justified
then she looks in my eyes
and guides them back to her optical level.

And its devilish
when she grants my wish
to make up time I missed
trying to play it off
as I checked out her ass
when she turned to cough
because all of a sudden she's developing asthma.

And its quite absurd,
those ridiculous curves
that she had the nerve
to press against me;

And its rotten luck
that I can't even touch
so much as a hair on her head
without getting excited.

But its quite alright
at the end of the night
because I just might get
a little closer tomorrow.

When I Pursue a Woman

It's bigger than she and I;
It is age-old and eternal; dating to the Eve of creation,
Ranging from the twinkle of her eyes to my emotions
exploding with supernova strength when I first met her.
It's also contextual in an universal language, so let me
explain it in Laymen's terms—

I yearn the one to whom I can pour out my heart,
From which her incinerating voice liquefies,
With astrological eyes reading my desires;
A soul mate,
Mind match,
And body mold;
Who controls my destiny in that my life's journey takes her
beside me;
With no other to suffice;
Ice cold contact from her feminine touch sending shivers
down my spine;
Congested cavities and air passages, suffocated by her
embrace;
Failed ventricles and pale as blood is extracted by the sight
of my Persephone;
Spirituality to lace my strength;
Patience, passionate understanding, and intelligence
melting every crevice of my cerebellum;
Well defined and my divine entity;
The better part of my entire being.

One Condition

The book of love possesses discrepancies—
Either that or love and faith together states a fallacy,
Because I've found that everything that leads me to believe love is on the way
Brings me to a dead end.
Should I follow the signs?
Well, the bull that was fed to me said that you're suppose to be all over me,
But that just gave me a bad taste of a Taurus.
I still don't have you in the palm of my hand.
Only then could you examine the patterns and read between the lines.
Listen.
From morning sessions to conversation we raced,
As to not miss meeting at our secret hiding place;
Making reservations to relax to a cartoon movie;
Spending hours corresponding the time away;
So long that it felt like days during the summer solstice.
I noticed that nothing grew out of this but a desire to make these idol plans;
And you never said no;
Not even the many insinuations, assumptions or innuendos drove you away;
Instead, maybe closer.
So tell me what barricades the days of our public display?
You know I respect your innocence and discipline,
And in the end do you think I want to come between you and Him?
You should know better.
I simply want to be a part of your world.
If you're still not convinced, keep listening.
It is not a performance to play the fool, it is genuine;

And you should know from the position that I'm in…think about it.
So trust me to approach the situation as gently as possible.
You should not fear a touch from me when this love is metaphysical.
I simply want to feel your soul;
To overcome the obstacles for us to grow a little more personal;
With one small condition that you can not refuse;
For me to introduce you to the real me.
Hi…I am love.

Daydreams

We sit side by side—
No words are said;
We barely make eye contact;
But in the back of our minds
We can both see ourselves
Connected to each other
In some fantastic manner;
Imaginary
But satisfying;
In a moment unrealized;
And hard to describe
Because in the blink of an eye,
Nothing is there.

Night Vision

Is this love or is this just what my mind is telling me?
Because my heart beats rapidly,
Rushing blood to my cheeks;
Blushing passionately whenever you pass by,
Blinding me with the sparkle in your eyes;
And those emerald beams are reminiscent of Oz
Through the epiphany that there is no place like home if
that is where you are.

And when I find you, I journey farther for new discoveries,
Unprotected and with no remorse;
My course is to enter into a wishful endeavor
With destination heaven as I part the gates.
Can you handle going there with me?

With my heart on my sleeve,
I hope to hold you by telling you that I love you,
But I settle by calling you my number one.
Yet I wonder where this leads,
Because I cannot see through the uncertainty even with
night vision;
My only light is you,
So tell me what is on your mind.

The Lady's Answer

I put this rhyme in rewind to remind me of this chorus I'm singing
From her class to her sass, she's got my mind ringing,
Locked in the words of this unchained melody;
Reversing the roles through subliminal signals, selling me on her verses sketched out in a love song;
Free-styled lines without rehearsals urging my participation.
She shows the existence of game in female species.
She makes these gentlemen look like gentle creatures;
Soothed in their savageness by the music of her bodily features;
Her movement keeps to the meter of my instrumental with me being at a loss of words;
But my eyes keep her rhythm from a distance.
The instance we lock eyes I catch a reprise of prior moments.
And she owns it like captured prey—the knowledge that I want her enticed by her flirtatious sway;
So contagious that I suffer from motion sickness;
Spinning out of control from the thickness and mystique of her physical nature;
And like forbidden fruit, I'm even captivated when ignored;
Hopelessly trying to explore the impossible truth that she is feeling me like I feel her.

F. L. O. W.

If you believe in love,
Let it lead your soul
To special leagues above
The need for control by emotional plugs;
Just let it flow

Pour it out to me,
My senses are open receptors
There's no pressure;
Why wait a lifetime when we're already here?

Love Theory

Our eyes made contact as love captured us,
Lifting us to the atmosphere of our feelings,
Orbiting the satellites, which are our hearts.

Sharing a common path,
We collide in celestial chaos.
But when the smoke clears, a new body is formed.

Our destiny is now in existence;
Our souls are unified with the commitment to one another.
We are one; we are love.

Love Law (Love Infinity)

Tender tendencies,
Gentle fantasies,
Tasty delicacies,
Combined mentalities,

Sweet sexuality,
In-depth journey,
Engulfed bodies
Sheer ecstasy.

Our minds set free
As our souls agree
Hearts pressed closely
No circulation be.

You and me
The two would be
Our destiny
To the degree of love…
…Infinitely.

How I Felt on 02-06-04
(On the Surface)

It's like stepping into mud holes or standing by the road in the rain
And getting soaked by an unconcerned driver—
In the cold, shivering to the bone on your long walk—umbrella blown inside out—
Having a deep desire to return home but perseverance pushes you forward until you get there—
Body saturated—all but your hair—making rhythms with the squishing sound of your socks like water spouts—
You get inside with nowhere to dry, and slide from your own collected precipitation—
Waiting for the day to roll by, but the time seems to run like molasses up an inclined plane—
But you remain in the greatest delight because despite the travel out, the return home to someone special is so magical—

That's how you make me feel.
You shield my heart from the harsh weather and internalize more pleasant conditions…

How I Felt on 02-06-04
(Deep Within)

I petition my flesh in yours as feelings pour through thoughts of your thickness
More than water for chocolate kisses upon your lips;
But I don't bother to stop the wishes that reality missed.
My spoken words rap upon your eardrum,
Penetrating your brain and pressing your lungs because I hear heavy breathing;
Leading me on the path of destructive diction,
Breaking down the will to resist as I mention methods to feed my desire;
You put my soul through the fire that burns bright in the light of your illuminating eyes; complemented by your smile.
You take me miles away from ordinary and that's why you are on my mind;
Making it so that I can't wait to return home.

When I Get You Alone

We remain at distant boundaries, but our hearts are on the same accord
As movement waits to manifest itself.
Until then, we stare, catching a vibe from soft music playing in the background,
Bound by the anxiety of what may materialize—
That being love, purified from the fact that despite indecision,
The new mission is to tempt the other into submission.
Then soon enough I become the facilitator.
With you beside me, I rub your arm tenderly to give you a feel of my friction,
Inviting the ignition of action through subliminal hints hid in warm conversation;
Sketching my strategy with a stroke of my fingers sending sweet sensations starting at your stomach,
Then sliding them to your waist and awaiting your response.
Slight sounds squeeze past your tense muscles;
Your breath barely above a whisper, high-pitched as whistling sighs ringing in love's melody;
Moisture condensing with misty eyes glistening in dim light,
Burning right through me; melting my resistance.
I move in with gentle continuance without pressing the issue;
Just staying patient as I read your body language.
It signals the release of love's energy as you taste my kiss, I kiss your lips, and then I reach your feet,
Completely consuming your sexual sentiments as passionate sustenance.

Feeling You

Sweet seductive aromas of your sexuality draws my heart into an obsessive rage
That I am drawn to you impulsively like unto a magnetic attraction.
Unwilling to fight temptations, my hands commence exploration,
Journeying the full horizon of your body, leaving no secrets of your being.
My body segregates as each limb stakes its own personal claim of you.
My lips conquer yours in a passionate kiss;
Generating a sensation arising from the fruit or your beauty.
My tongue engages in the struggle, yearning a single taste of your heavenly presence.
Simultaneously, my fingers continue to conquer your emotions
As you slowly guide them around every curve,
Exposing treasures that lay vulnerable of my capture.
My heart sends out signals indicating the desire of engagement from my chest.
You answer the call, saturating it in kisses, exciting my most inner infatuations.
As I take you in my arms your body turns limber as to surrender to my advances.
I find myself in the midst of your deepest affection
And both our souls start to encounter the burn of our desires for one another.
As we travel deeper into erotic yearnings, such sensation intensifies;
That to our physical beings it injects an instantaneous chill.
In response pours bodily vapors, cascading our entangled anatomy.

I lay drowned in admiration with one explanation for my enchantment—
I am feeling you.

Acts of Nature

I speak in the softest verse to gently capture your mind.
I massage each limb of your blossoming nature,
Slowly,
Generating a feel for my affection.
As you speak, I absorb all delectable diction with a passionate kiss,
And our words roll from my tongue to yours,
Imitating fruit freshly extracted from the most righteous vines.
As we both taste our intensions, we sense the sweet moments arising from our playful mood.

Continuing in our exploits, I take you as my queen,
Carry you to your royal suite, and proceed to pay my loyalty in your name.
My arms being your throne, I wrap you up, admiring the silky gown of faint lavender,
Revealing a glimpse of the alms of your profound sexuality—
Standing as the next wonder of the world—
And I play the caretaker as I take measures of preservation.
Carefully I work the contours of your shrine to maintain your smooth anatomy.
My tender touch is evaporated through each open pour,
Penetrating into your bloodstream; initiating your highness.
Addicted to all our your royal pleasure, your voice vibrates in a demanding tone,
Your body dictating my hands through each of its palatial cavities.
As being a servant to your adoration, I submit to my respectful position,
Offering full attributions with the touch of my lips to the bounds of your bodily extremities.

The overflow of emotions creates an inner tension sending an instantaneous chill throughout your body.
Deep contractions as of seismic vibrations rupture an orgasmic cataclysm
That bursts in the midst of our somatic covalence.
The flames of our heated passion consume us;
Lying;
Staring;
With the yearning of once more being engulfed.

As We Continue – The Morning After

You shine through my window as the alarm on the dawn of my awakening
Taking me from this reality on the wings of a fantasy;
You and me, suspended in attraction
Attached through covalent limbs
Sending love through the exchange of bodily fluid
Receiving lashes from continuous motion—my up and down with no interruption
Holding the reigns to keep control of the emotions until it's over;
Your hands hold my shoulders as you kick away the cover until we reach full exposure,
Overflowing with love, time slowly rolls
Then…orgasm and slumber is greeted by a kiss on your stomach before I turn over.
Rest.
You will need it as we continue

The Climax

I took one last chance,
Last dance,
On the last record;

The last hour,
Last minute,
Last second;

For the last aroma,
Last look,
Last wish,
The last time a woman makes me feel like this;

The last hug,
Last kiss,
Last sensation,
Last proposal of a private invitation;

Last touch,
Last taste,
Last breath,
The last moment before there's nothing left—
—because there's nothing greater than loving you to death.

Disconnected

Hey love,
Come go with me through my mental fields,
So I can show you that how I really feel has me sprung like wild flowers pervading emerald hills.
Yet, still you are not convinced with what I have to say.
But, wait…let me go on.
Since the conversation is over the phone
And my words are being transformed into electric impulses,
Let me add my own voltage;
Even though the flow of my affection is not measurable in Watts.
But a humidity of 98% satisfies the meter,
As the vapors rise from your hot bath, soaking your sweet skin like herbal tea.
I take a sip as I await dessert to be served in a simple pleasure, brand name Nature's Finest.
Then removing you from your china, I take you by one hand with the other on your waist
As I guide you to our secret place; with no vacancies except for love.
Then I'll case your body; searching the tender spots;
Making your mind the melting pot of passion and temptation.
And I'll keep right there for a while,
You smiling as I tease you with a soft touch and a sudden stop;
Testing you to the point that you seem to explode;
Then I continue with a massage to smooth the flow.
Having your eyes rolling with heavy sighs because you know this is where it all begins.
But in disappointment, as is my reply; since my desires are fenced in imaginary boundaries

If you are not convinced that what I have to say is true;
And it all remains just a thought; disconnected from reality.

The Seasons Haiku

Love will Spring forth a
Summer crush that will Fall in
The dead of Winter.

The Present Matters

What do I do…?
When I can't love someone enough to make them stay?
And my stubbornness can't let them walk away?

I want to be relieved of these feelings, yet they drill in me.
Leaving me open to submission,
I heed to uncertainty that this time I will stand my ground
As I lay down my convictions when you whisper,
"I just want to be with you."

What do I do…?
When jealousy eats at my soul and it should not be an option?
Then I feel as if we COULD—if we tried—go back without repercussion.

But,
My best does not add up;
My all falls short;

Still I shed reality for a dream
Even though it seems bad for your health and sanity;
Wounded by the notion that it simply cannot be;
And no matter the length of the sword, it cuts just as deep;
Making my heart bleed dry of caring.

My Love Theme

Its one of the things about love that you just cannot explain
The stress and strain;
Tripping out;
The blame;
Reconciliation and repetition;
Vicious cycles;
Recycling heart tissue;
Regeneration of lost pride;
Long rides and train wrecks;
Calamity and discord from this melody…

Baby I love you but I…
I have to do my own thing.
But if we become butterflies in the next lifetime,
We can fly over the rainbow.

Too bad the rain pours;
The water stain's old;
It's from that same old first line;
How's that refrain goes?

We come to terms with the reality;
That this love was just a fallacy;
Mathematically we didn't add up;
The current era never had us;
But face it, we only have now;
We're not guaranteed reincarnation;
But she's hell bent on waiting;
Singing her song as justification;

Baby I love you but I…
I have to do my own thing.
But if we become butterflies in the next lifetime,

We can fly over the rainbow.

Too bad the rain pours;
The water stain's old;
It's from that same old first line;
How's that refrain go?

Tomorrow isn't promised, it's only assumed;
For us become butterflies we must start our cocoon;
Compatible with provisions of cohabitation;
No hesitation;
But too soon you try to sing away my desires;
But don't realize there's no harmony in your tune;

Baby I love you but I...
I have to do my own thing.
But if we become butterflies in the next lifetime,
We can fly over the rainbow.

Too bad the rain pours;
The water stain's old;
It's from that same old first line;
How's that refrain goes?

Why I Kept Calling

Fresh sheets and crisp linens are greeted with grins of being dedicated to your attention;
As I lie on my bed deep in conversation;
The blood rushing to my face;
With smiles paining my muscles from the strain of the blushing;
Rushing to meet the chime of the off-peak hours to make that connection;
Even from afar I feel you consume my soul into yours;
The rain pours and we do not feel it.
Weathered wishes have long since come true;
"She's the one," whispers my mind in a sidebar.
Ridiculous subjects follow silence.
Then secret moments of future expectations and sudden sighs from an unknown source
Creates the soul searching rendition of truth or dare;
Both enquiring to become aware of hidden feelings.
And all is spilled and collected in the memory pot as correspondence turns to ordinary;
But inside, the outcome has been tolled;
One being sold from the response but still struggling with the notion that love has not been proclaimed in the desired fashion;
Trying to remain rational, I fix my response to soothe her reaction,
Though subconsciously lashing out at the world that the one could not be mine;
But there's always tomorrow, I think to myself.
Then I move to Plan B.

Why I Haven't Called in a While

I was falling for you, but what can I do when you were not there to catch me?
You write me off to fate's possession,
Scratch through my profession,
And discarded my heart.
So I guess you are the queen—
Because tears from your tyranny have me submerged in a river of regret
That I let you control so much of me;
I was too blind to see that there was no definition to this relationship.
I think about what I would have given you, given up, and left behind for a lifetime of living in your presence.
The lessons taught me that love is just another emotion.
I love as much as I hate, loath and mourn—but I will bounce back in the morning.
So I take this as a lesson learned; I've earned another stripe—
Another element of strife is wiped from my shoulders.
I cannot hold on to what does not have a firm foundation.
So I'm vacating the premises and taking what's left of my dignity.

Anti-Social

Simple realities played out in my mind forms a complex web that holds the answers to the tears I shed and the life I lead.

Materialistic love has its framework on my heart.
It holds me to want, to desire, to fiend love,
Which momentarily shine its lustful rays of pleasure and stains its memories in the passed time that has now been extracted from my existence.
I wallow in the feeling of regret for such a minuscule hope…but deep inside me, I long for such attention infinitely.

My cravings increasing, I persistently travel to new heights of personal despair; creating seeds of undue hardships and then contemplating the unholy thought of destroying all evidence of my moral misdeeds. My corrupt judgments lead me in the cycle that has been the grave of my pure feelings.

Yet from the flames of my internal conflict arises a cloud of calm.
I stand firm to the mental infirmities; not to be destroyed by such unnecessary constraints as love and friendship.
My idol mind controls my destiny and rejects an accomplice.
Likewise, solitude devours my soul as my heart longs for companionship.

Why I'm not the Perfect Guy

I have always been infatuated by the opposite sex,
Growing up dominated and now tolerating this overrated respect;
Being frustrated by it not being enough to want her mind, body, spirit and soul;
Not to control,
Just to mend, mold, caress, and hold them, inches away from eternity.
It is so close but not a reality.
There is no approach from fearing rejection;
I try to lose the ego but it is stuck in my throat;
Too hard to swallow my pride, I hide and gloat at how nonchalantly I move to the next that shows potential.
When all I wanted was that one chance.
Behind the masquerade, it brings me pain.
But not once did my mind entertain playing games.
It only takes one person to satisfy me.
And it is not hard to gain my love;
Just she remain in the same mind frame as the world in which I picture—
A portrait painted richer than the bold glow of Van Gogh's *Starry Nights*.
A perfect delight and happiness with no compromise,
Except for me to lose myself in your eyes and in your affection;
Deserted in the abyss of love with no rescue.
But it seems too much to ask.
The truth is masked by drastic pre-conceived ideas and misrepresentations.
It seems that I am an untrusting, African American Aquarius, and left-handed.
While your Mr. Right takes you in the opposite direction of his persona.

And you still find me around at those tender moments trying to keep you going.
Yet my total dedication shows that the best is never enough.
I guess that's why I'm not the perfect guy.

My Love in Return

My love in return is tenfold its beginnings,
For I knew not the tender moments drawn in the past.
Now the things that used to be are the things that I am longing;
To return to the love once overflowing.
It streamed through two hearts converged into a common vascular flow;
Creating a fork that tenderized my soul.
Now to have my passionate pastries,
And tasting the luscious qualities of your fruitful being is an unrealized dream.
I stand at the edge of my affections, aspiring to fall to the former depths,
Wishing that your love will come to my rescue; reviving the things that could have been.

Presently hoping, fearing, loving each ancient memory,
I feel that now the foundation has reconstructed away from what used to be sentimental,
And I desire to stir exuberant thoughts with my words, my voice, and my lips.
But how can I explain the things that I must say to reincarnate our departed souls
When my words seem to be planted on barren grounds;
Leaving me to hold on to abstract hope; making me an empty vessel, singing out to you
With a single inquiry plaguing my heart--"Does she accept my love?"

My Love in Return
How can I explain myself when I know that your love for me is gone?

I'm all alone wanting you for myself; you can tell it by the simple things I do.
And I do… I do love you and I want to wrap you in these arms of mine for all times.
I'm wanting you.

Feeling You Still

I want to feel the affection that I'm missing,
Acting as a shield and protection through the hugs, the kisses and your touch;
I don't ask for much,
But I'm willing to give anything for the assurance you bring amidst my insecurities.
Purity pervades these wishes; placing my heart as collateral;
In a literal sense, I put my word on everything I own
That you mean more to me than I care to confess;
Contested by acts to suppress it
With desperate attempts to down-play what I can't deny is infatuation;
My true feelings rest branded upon my chest
As the permanent mark you left upon my soul
With uncontrollable impulses causing me to fidget as you the enter the room;
I avoid situations to be close to you when all I want is to be really close to you;
We both could use the escape into our own world.

Oh, how I want the gift to read your mind
And be mystified that we think along the same lines;
Both searching to find the place deep within our spirits
That longs for intervention with the physical realm
You falling under my spell as I stir in my black magic;
Not to speak heresy but express the intimacy of this engagement;
But holding patience as a virtue, I wait;
Facing the fact that I'm still feeling you,
But placing those emotions aside for someone else.

LSD (Love So Deep)

Just like my first experience in the streets,
Your love reminds me of LSD.
But it's this love so deep inside of me that has turned me into a fiend.
Its like paradise prescribed with opium utopias;
My nasal passages congested with my angel's dust.
Lack luster beams gleam in my eyes glazed over.
Inhaling your aroma collapses my lungs like smoke filled rooms;
I am consumed with the fire of desire, ignited by passion;
Hallucinogens flirt with my endorphins;
I overdose and welcome the after-life.

Taken

I have you in my attention;
Detained you to my intentions;
To take you in the middle of my mental visions;

Provisions are invitation
To incisions of sensation
Initiating treatment to anatomical temptations.

Feminine indentations suppressed by the engagement
Are pressed with the notion of a subversive motion,
Submerged in ocean currents with navigation fluent
Maneuvering through fluid reaction to sublevel locations.

Low vibrations and ripples and waves of circular motion
Moves emotion center to sexual mutation.
Metamorphosis of conversation to unified conversions,
Fuses the ignition of spontaneous satisfaction.

My Paradise

If I could describe my paradise, it would be a simple life in a simple world;
Boy and girl escaping to the seashore to dance in the crashing waves;
On-looking the lighthouse standing pure white;
A fresh ocean breeze circulates every night.
Celestial lights illuminate the space beyond the pier.
God's music plays in our ears, orchestrated by the nocturnal life.
No worries. No fears.
Not even time wasted waiting to cast a wish upon falling stars,
Because there is more potential of a dream coming true under the ones heavily suspended.
Happily ever after is never-ending when the fairytale becomes life;
Because its paradise being with you
And I'm in it.

I. C. U.

You're so contagious that I can't escape this epidemic;
Being infected with this sickness the moment of contact.
I caught the bug at first sight and every night since then my condition has worsened;
First I awake with cold chills but realize that my temperature's high;
My misty eyes give rise to hallucinations.

With my sight fading, I vaguely hear my name and wonder if I'm going to see the light;
Through the bright flashes of my life.
I feel hands on my shoulders and I know that it is almost over.
I feel my soul slipping into a place undiscovered;
I'm covered in a natural dress and resting in a piece of heaven.

The Truth about Relationships

Yeah, we walked the straight line but we fell off
Plunged to the love bungee and the lines got crossed
Wish I had known before the bouquet was tossed
That its destination was my grave at love's cost.

Yeah, we walked the straight line be we staggered
I guess hiding intoxication was not mastered
Now like the walls that confine me, I'm plastered;
Left to suffer for my feelings, a lonely bastard.

Yeah we walked the straight line but it turned.
I was thrown a curveball that caught me in the sternum
Now I'm scarred by the game and left burned.
Becoming a victim of love's cremation is what I earned.

Yeah we walked the straight line but I slipped.
I fell head over heals in a ditch.
I had scuffmarks on my Nikes and a broken stitch.
I realized that she tripped me… "Old nasty bitch!"

The New Years' Eve

"Now I seem to understand.
You're just the New Years' Eve
Scheming on a man to destroy God's plan."

Dangerous curves ahead are possessed by her body;
Hypnotizing the weakest brothers to meet their fate.

Her luscious red-rose lips seem as delicate as a flower;
A source of her power you get to know too late.

And oh! Don't let her put that appeal on you—you'll never escape.
Then she'll seal your fate with a kiss of death.

She'll have you begging for more, just long enough to work her magic;
Making you call on her—begging for mercy with your last breath.

"I've been onto you since you began.
You're just the New Years' Eve
Scheming on a man to destroy God's plan."

She's a human epidemic; seeking whom she may devour.
Her voice so tantalizing it will make you come to your final hour.

In the beginning she used an apple; trapping man by fulfilling his need.
Some still choose to eat today, a power she thinks will never sour.

From first sin to the end; death comes to all who enter her presence.
She's the devil with a fine body and evil in her eyes.

To bring men to their knees is what brings her pleasure.
She takes any measures to make sure the garden in forever filled with cries.

"But you won't catch this man.
You're just the New Years' Eve
Scheming on a man to destroy God's plan."

Long Eyes

Left to right the wrongs, I write
So that I do not fail, but sail over the assailant to the crimes of my heart;
Since lights from my shining star is reflected to a different source.
I take the stripes on the this late night and come back twice as hard;
The steak knife breaks right at impact with my back shielded with Teflon;
The great white is all hype because all hope is gone;
The emotional rollercoaster is so repetitive that I could copyright this sad song;
But I stay strong,
Shedding this grief through these long eyes.

My Poem Cry

I bear down hard to make the ink smear when I scribe—
With my pen I make the poem cry.
The only moisture comes from the fresh words
Because it is like a desert in my eyes.

Are you surprised at my composure or more surprised that I wouldn't hold you?
So that you could get your closure after closing the door on my heart?
Now that we're apart its better; forget the weather; I bear a tough shelter;
Shielding my feelings and showing no reaction;
Because if you see me break down it might give you the satisfaction.
But with every lash I receive for my passion, you can only imagine who has the last laugh in the end.
With teeth gnashing, you've got to grin and bear it;
Because apologies don't repair quickly enough.
I might be a little sick but I've got a tough immune system;
Things shouldn't have come to this if I had followed common wisdom—
"Once they're gone, forget them. It's their fault that they left—
But I placed that aside because I thought we had something special.
Now I know that love is just here to test you, and test the weight of your spirit.
And I have to hand to you, nice try.
The one time you made me cry, I took it outside—
The tears got lost in the rain like my heart got lost in the pain—
On my face are not water spots, its more like blood stains.

My pride still remains and I don't blame you, I'm above you.
I just came down on your level; tried to be down for whatever;
But you pulled me down in the gutter.
However, I'm tough as leather so I'm moving on without a stutter in my voice or in my step;
And taking back the little contentment I have left because…

I bear down hard to make the ink smear when I scribe—
With my pen I make the poem cry.
The only moisture comes from the fresh words
Because it is like a desert in my eyes.

Be happy. You just made it in another dedication.

No Grudges

I think it's about time I really told what happened.
It was very cold how the episode ends.
If it would re-run, I'm running from the memories.
Sometimes you have to face the past, but not me.
Three years facing the storms we were together, however,
We couldn't stand the summer weather.
When things got a little heated we would boil over.
Yet, on the inside our hearts grew colder.
Till someone else radiated their heat.
That was the straw that made me toss your ass in the street.
However, it wasn't that easy. It took a lot of inner struggle to really make me leave.
And the lies to cover infidelity pull back, full of self-pity,
And self-doubt of character for abandoning you,
But all the time the words you spoke weren't really true.
My facial expressions resembled old rags just from the fact of being had.
But being too mixed with feelings to be upset,
I just laid it all down and walked away—folded my bet.
Just hoping in a few years it would be kosher,
But too many memories bring the nightmare closer.
And yet I don't regret it any longer
Because what don't drive you insane only makes you stronger.
Now I'm even more powerful and wise,
Watching with both eyes, scoping through the disguise,
Cautious and attentive for the rest of my life.
Be proud, you taught me well.

In Time...

In time, the wounds will heal;
Because I'm getting immune to the feeling;
But steel hurts with stakes taken in the heart so many times,
Yet it still builds the rhyme that flows so strongly from my mind,
Through my heart to my limbs;
Through pens to my pad;
Sadness rushing to the ballpoint as I confront reality in structured motion;
Left to right to write what is left of the pain;
And abstain from destructive composure.

Visions of Rapture

We all have our take on life and most agree that it doesn't treat us right;
Wondering if there is a need to fight it;
Pledging allegiance to hold the strife close to my heart;
And made to believe that it's a right;
But when it bleeds, who makes it alright and who holds the knife?
Or are they just one in the same?
Or do we all share in the blame?
Because we claim that we share in pain;
Even though we travel different planes;
Some soaring and some getting caught up in the world trade;
Like it's been gotten from the mind of bin Laden; but we've been plotting our own downfall.
It's like we hate ourselves and its no better when we get older;
That's why you can never find me sober;
Trying to distort reality to transform it around my goggle vision.

I knew a girl who let the pressures around her close in;
Until she had no room for friends;
So packed tightly that she couldn't see over; didn't know love rested on her shoulders
With wide open arms to hold her to keep her warm so her heart grew colder;
And I told her that I was everything that she needs,
But I don't know why the pain still collects in her eyes;
You can't disguise strength with foolish pride;
I didn't want to be a ruler or guide; just a confident to help ease the ride
While rolling shotgun beside her;

You only got one life to live; one love to give
That is made of pure emotion; the rest is hoping for fulfillment to voids;
Which can only be filled by God;
But we still rely on ourselves, making our lives a living hell,
And the price of bail is our soul;
One precious piece that I hope to hold until my days of old.
So that I reach the rays of gold that reach from the sky.
No more signing a lease but inheriting my place in heaven.
And cop a plea that my past be irrelevant;
When I indulged in at least three of the seven deadly sins;
I would have severed heads for friends or broken commandments,
But in the end I'm the one condemned; I can't be saved by them;
So what's the worth of the risk?
Not enough to continue so I stick to my own venues,
Looking for visions of rapture to take my soul to the life after.

Marooned Visions

She will be loved, even if it's not by me;
However the need to be is mutual because she feeds my securities,
Surpasses my self-conscious criticisms,
And meets my arrogance with proportionate cynicism.
She's the protagonist in my seemingly fairytale, but with the fairly well-to-do ending;
Since her heart is still mending;
Yet appending threads attach hers to mine; having me hoping not to cause a run.

We look for sunsets and daisies but only get the occasional clear skies;
Leaving us wandering through clouds cast over other days;
Trying to get back to where we were, we realize that we are going in circles.
All we know is that our orbit sends us free-falling to a center point of despair;
And this remedy is a paradox when love consists of taking such a plunge.

It would be easy if she heeded to my calling,
But the beating of my heart cannot tap out the correct code to connect our souls.
So I remain distant because I know that she will be loved…
…Even if it's not by me.

Words Never Said...

Words never said may seem impossibly heard, yet are unnecessary because I want to feel these words flow through you as naturally as the blood through your veins; Let the syllables flood your reaction to incite the attraction of your attention to my agenda.
My only purpose is to keep you here so that I can embrace away your anxieties.
I know life is not that easy, but anything is conquerable with love on your side.
And if left unsaid, actions can carry emotion; as do my deeds hold this notion like the wings of a dove holds the soul on its final journey to heaven.
You are love; you are the very reason for the disintegration of my fears, and the composition of my tears as your beauty compresses my sight at the ducts; making misty eyes every moment that I behold your precious face.
And the sweet nectar of your kiss nurtures my spirit to immortal bliss as I wish that these feelings will never die.
I catch tremors from deep inside and realize that I'm filled with more than butterflies, but more like fairies;
And not even a thousand of their wishes granted can put me as high as I soar with you as the source of my elevation.
I desire to take you through the full scope of my emotions but I don't obligate to stay around.
However, I am glad that you are still here.
I don't know what the future holds, but in it we are well suspended.
With you, I can challenge even the uncharted territory reached by me feeling so deeply.
And I hope that you can see all that I have said because it had been left unspoken.
You have left me open to new ambitions in life.
And by the reigns of this ride, I will take grip.

Like a baby pacified to peace, I hold your name upon my lips.
"Josephine," you are to me perfection so don't ever change.
And with this being written, I close with it stained as witness to these…
…words never said…
I love you.

A Lifetime

If not for a lifetime, then at least a moment could I own my destiny;
Instead of sitting here desperately,
Down on one knee,
Begging for the blessing of being the one you need and desire.

What is worse is how helplessly I watch as others take the breath from you,
Constraining your heart from the oxygen that is your happiness
As they suffocate you with their so-called love;
And if there is none greater than a man lay down his life for another,
Then why do they try to take yours?

I wish I could protect you.
I would take the best times that you've had and place them in a chest
To preserve the good and shield away the bad.
But with each minute that passes by,
Time takes chance out of my hand and places it in an hourglass,
Turning my hopes to sand;
And in the end, the only gains we stand to claim is withstanding the pain and pressure
To the degree that the wasted grains produce diamonds.

And in that instance, we might be happy
If only could I own my destiny—
If not for a lifetime…then at least a moment.

Rose Petals for Josephine

I see you as such an amazing person who deserves the best in life,
From love to service of your every need,
Never even having to lift a finger to feed your beautiful body;
I want to be the one that gives you all that your heart desires and things forgotten;

But I've remained in silence because I felt that I never had enough to suffice;
I couldn't sacrifice the perfect moment with an inferior attempt at capturing your heart;

I've remained in silence because once the word were said,
I wished to shower you with the evidence in multitudes of diamond-cut promises;
But I was a poor, helpless, hopeless romantic falling in love;

Now, late nights I lie in silence, no longer lullibied by your soft voice and gentle touch;
And having nightmares of destroying the love that I hoped to build;
With no foundation to place these feelings and speak acceptance in your heart, they fell through.

But let me steal the opportunity to make things right.
You captured my heart on the spot and from there I've fallen deeply for you.
You had me from "hello," will destroy me with "goodbye," but can save me with this one chance.
I will always love you and I hope that you can love me, too.

I still remember when you told me that you didn't want it to end just yet;
Neither do I;
That's why I sit here picking rose petals for luck in this love.

A Bit of Wishful Thinking

If it was up to me, you'd be my girl
And we would waste time away talking about how we hope
to stay together
Making future plans but only…and I quote,
"If we make it there,"
Setting limits on the vision but still looking to the horizon;
Wishing that the "beyond" was set like auburn suns at
dusk;
In each other we trust like Gods among men;
Not letting in the mythology of the storytellers
Set out on an odyssey to interfere in our alignment;
Let us keep stars shining in our eyes
Reminding us of the treasure buried within;
But we have to begin to see our way through.

I love liking you and would like to love you if it's right;
Believe too that despite the read through,
I'll recite the need to find the path that leads to nights
That me and you might meet at the moon and remain
weightless;
So high that we can't be grounded;
Surrounded by love
And founded by love
Pounding through the heartbeats in rhythms and melodies.

And I try to settle the debt by pitching pennies in a well
And hope time will tell through word that you're his
offspring.

You Simply Are...

You simply are the most incredible being
Brushed across the canvas of life's portrait;
Picture-perfect and pure;
Taking shape of an entity never previously imagined by the mortal mind;
Can no other find such a treasure that is so simply amazing;
Graced upon my life and how sweet it sounds;
Be that I found what I have searched for
Through desert lands and destitute;
And it is simply you who are a part of the dream that nurtures my thoughts to a world of fantasy;
Delightfully beautiful and delectable;
Possessed with a delicate touch that accesses my affections;
You are the very element of nature
Laced with the greens of vegetation
And I do not hesitate to partake in the creation
Who could only by produced by the hands of God.

I try hard to visualize life absent of your presence
And it simply cannot be conceived;
For I believe in destiny; that it might be you and I escaping to a new life;
You are simply what I live my life to achieve;
A love that holds more power than a lightning strike twice in the same destination;
It all a simply impossibility to re-occur so I cherish you;
And would down my life and perish through as many deaths as it takes
To recreate the life that we had started this now distance eon. You are beyond the timeless love that I had wished for; More than wonderful;
Taking me under with my desires burning, soul searing,
And spiritually yearning simply...you.

Unconventional

Call me unconventional because I steer away from the being labeled the typical;
My touch remains metaphysical;
Going beyond the surface to make a holistic love;
It is no analytical approach to go through because my true devotion will soak through your soul;
I may not fit the mold because it was broken;
I'm self-contained and will always remain unconventional;
I still can keep the traditional—
Down on one knee after I rescue you in a fairytale;
But soon after, you must humble down too so that we see eye to eye;
That we function on the same level facing obstacles and go through them together;
And we will never lose focus or concentration;
My imperfections cannot be matched with my dedication;
I never stray from being faithful; playing into expectations in unseen manners;
I put my attention on your pleasure and satisfaction that may cause reaction to which you are not accustomed—
A custom made through innovative ways from me being labeled unconventional.

Untitled (Cyberchat)

When I saw you, I melted instantly
Having my mind convincing me that you were a mirage
So I wiped my eyes to remove the image,
But it remained steadfast
And like stained glass separating light to colorful rays,
The sight of you separated my thoughts
As I gazed at my masterpiece
Thinking that you have to be beyond this world's creation;
Maybe heavenly;
So can I convince destiny to align the path for us to meet,
Or should I agree with my mind,
Which surely believes that you are unreal.

Volatile Affections

She was more than I hoped or thought was possible;
Possessing affections that I found to be volatile;
Now I'm desperately battling for a love that melts my heart to molecules;
Facing obstacles to withstand the heat.

She's the type that can make me put my life on the line;
Ignoring the signs that may say "wrong way"
Because when I see her, it feels so right;
Harms' way is the straight and narrow in my eyesight;
Just from the hope that I might get close enough for her touch.
I am vexed to see what direction I will go with a love of such potency;
Yet I hold on; as it seems my heart is going to explode;

More than mercury rises as temperatures soar;
As my soul is incinerated in a sentimental inferno;
Wildly burning with a passion that consumes every inch of my being;
Leaving my unrecognizable as my former self;

I have fallen further into a depth that went over the edge of physical perception;
I now sense her spirit penetrating through my body as I absorb her volatile affections.

Got Me Looking So Crazy in Love

Trying to go smoothly,
You said, "Don't rush the flow,"
But steadily I fell as easily as the fall breeze crept in
To season the days with a mild relaxation;

So I took the tempo from take it slow to just making it;
Marinating love won't soak in if we can't make it last forever;

I could not sever ties when my affections tied a knot in my stomach
To trap the butterflies whenever my eyes were cast upon your smile;

I think about us
And feel and breathe the hope of seeing the pictures in my head as reality;
Surrendering to the weakness that leaves me falling apart;

Instead of trying to get my life back together,
I rather start one with you;
But it goes beyond say;
We must work our way to the creation of a relationship born as destiny's child.

Right Here, Right Now

It's a little too early to catch the ripeness
But a little too late for me to fight this
So I write this off as just another lesson in life
But how can it be wrong when it feels so right?

Baby, just conceal the light
So that we can do it in the shadows
That as we get closer,
We only cast one ghost
Upon the haunting truth of what is going on

And with feelings so strong,
It's like we belong in this place
I see compliance written on your face
Of the defiant way we fool the naked eye
With hidden engagement underneath blatant playfulness

And how long I waited to finally arrive at this place;
It won't be long before we are on our way to ecstasy
Especially because I feel we deserve it
But we have to deal with the urges
While they are still accessible
And right now it seems that our timing is impeccable.

Window to the Soul

I imagine you in sunny melodies;
Rays and notes flowing through;
Intertwined in vivid memories;
Seeing smiles light love, hugs and playful moments;
Back and forth in flirtatious traits of conversation;
Wave after wave are feelings layered on my heart
As I take part in this engagement;
It is so amazing how we sustain this attraction;
More than infatuation plays a role;
It's the way the souls combine to one body;
There's a lot we have to accomplish;
If we want this to blossom;
Can it be possible that we go to a place where love is free flowing;
From stream through veins to spirit;
Where we don't have to talk to hear it—we feel it;
And it draws us closer as float towards the gate
And await entrance into the enchanted lands;
Greater than that of milk and honey;
A land where we can explore all uncertainties
As we'll be rulers of our own destiny;
Destined to be in love.

ABOUT THE AUTHOR

Nigel Walker was born February 13, 1980 to Jacqueline and David Walker. He was born and raised in Eufaula, AL by his mother along with seven brothers and sisters. He has been writing poetry since he was about 11 years old and continues today to paint vivid pictures through the expressions of poetry.

Nigel began writing in a way to mimic the works of some of his greatest influences such as Robert Frost, John Donne, Edgar Allan Poe, among others. However through the struggles of growing up in a single parent home and in public housing, his poetry was personalized as an outlet of the many emotions he felt during the times and trials of his life. It is true to the day that his poetry can be seen as a direct reflection of his life and personality, even though some are fictionalized to a certain extent.

His works have been published in several literary magazines, such as *Early Spring*, the *Menagerie*, and the *Scroll*. He has also received acclaim in various poetry contests such as Poetry.com. He has made several public performances, including a guest performance for Stess the Emcee, who opened for Cee-lo in concert on the campus of LaGrange College; and serving a regular at LaGrange College's Spoken Word session called the *Cypher*. He also appeared in an Independent Artist showcase at the former Club Shine in Atlanta, GA.

His first book published was a collection of romantic dedication poems entitled *The Secret Diaries of Jean B*atiste was debuted in 2004. *Rose Petals for Josephine* is his second published book of poetry, which adds a fictional love interest to the fictionalized character, Jean Batiste, who was created in the first work. It add a more intimate look into the author by attempting chronicle the relationship with one of women to whom a poem was dedicated in the first book.

www.ingramcontent.com/pod-product-compliance
Lightning Source LLC
LaVergne TN
LVHW051158080426
835508LV00021B/2696